SEX

What's God got to do with it?

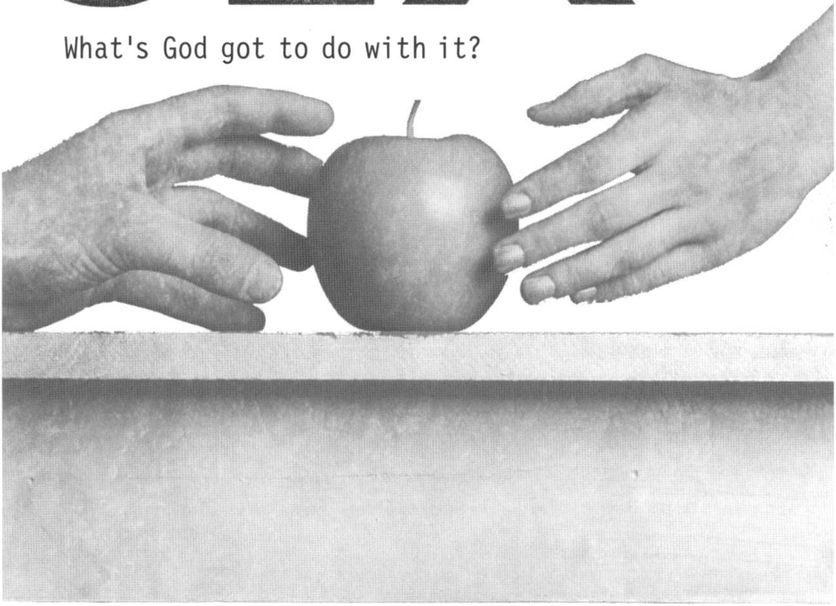

SIX SESSIONS

With Notes for Leaders

RICK RICHARDSON

InterVarsity Press
Downers Grove, Illinois

These guides are dedicated to
the staff of InterVarsity Christian Fellowship
and of the Axis ministry of Willow Creek Community Church
whose hearts are big enough to want to
show and share God's love with the next generation.

InterVarsity Press
P.O. Box 1400, Downers Grove, IL 60515-1426
World Wide Web: www.ivpress.com
E-mail: mail@ivpress.com

InterVarsity Press® is the book-publishing division of InterVarsity Christian Fellowship/USA®, a student movement active on campus at hundreds of universities, colleges and schools of nursing in the United States of America, and a member movement of the International Fellowship of Evangelical Students. For information about local and regional activities, write Public Relations Dept., InterVarsity Christian Fellowship/USA, 6400 Schroeder Rd., P.O. Box 7895, Madison, WI 53707-7895, or visit the IVCF website at <www.ivcf.org>.

Cover design: Rick Devon

Photo image: Mark Fiorenzo

ISBN 0-8308-2026-4

Printed in the United States of America ∞

P 17 16 15 14 13 12 11 10 9 8 7 6 5 4 3 2 1
Y 15 14 13 12 11 10 09 08 07 06 05 04 03 02

CONTENTS

INTRODUCTION
WHAT'S GOD GOT TO DO WITH IT?

We live in a day of sexual stimulation. We are bombarded with sexual images twenty-four hours a day, and most people in our culture have come to the conviction that whatever consenting adults agree to sexually is fine.

We live in a day of sexual experimentation. Many in our culture decide to live together before they get married in order to determine if they are sexually compatible. And people today believe it is their right to experience sexual satisfaction. One popular song depicts sex as the great healing experience.

We also live in a day of sexual manipulation. Sex is used to sell everything from cars to deodorant. Sexual attractiveness is power, and the movies and television use sex to pump up their ratings. A recent study found twenty thousand scenes of suggested sexual intercourse or other sexual behavior documented in a single year of prime time.

But the freedom arising out of the sexual revolution in the sixties hasn't delivered all it seemed to promise. Sexual abuse, date rape, STDs and the painful aftermath of broken relationships have led many to think there must be more to the story.

I am convinced that in order to achieve true sexual fulfillment, we must also achieve solid sexual integrity. Our bodies and our souls, our commitments and our relationships, our self-worth and our sexual experiences must all be integrated. When sex is looked at as only physical, when we experience sexual connection without intimacy, and give ourselves away in experiences that undermine our own sense of dignity and self worth, we will not achieve sexual fulfillment. Sexual fulfillment and sexual integrity go together.

In this guide, we will be discussing how people today can find both sexual integrity and sexual fulfillment. And we will be looking at the wisdom the Bible has to offer in that search.

What's God got to do with it? Our hope is that as we see some of the many links between our spirituality and our sexuality, our bodies and our souls, our hearts and our passions, we will grow toward greater sexual integrity and fulfillment.

So let's begin!

The Groups Investigating God Series

The Groups Investigating God series was developed based on the conviction that your spiritual journey is unique and that your questions are important.

Too many of us grew up in a spiritual environment where only certain kinds of questions were valued.

These guides are especially for you if you have spiritual and life questions that you want to be able to ask and discuss and explore without fear of being judged or feeling intimidated. They are for you whether you consider yourself a skeptic or a seeker, religious or nonreligious. These guides are designed to offer help in finding spiritual wisdom for real-life issues.

What Part Does the Bible Play?

Why do we use the Bible in these discussions? Because we have found it to be a book full of wisdom for anyone who takes the time to engage with it. You don't have to "believe in the Bible" to have a great time with these discussions. You only have to be willing to see what wisdom it might shed on life's great issues.

The playing field is level. Bible passages are printed in the guide itself, so you don't have to feel intimidated by not knowing where things are.

We especially try to engage with some of the wisdom of Jesus, who was, by all accounts, one of the greatest teachers about spirituality and life who ever lived. Again, you don't need to "believe in Jesus" to get a lot out of these discussions, but just be open to the wisdom Jesus might have for your life.

How to Use These Guides

You can certainly use these guides on your own and benefit a great deal. The questions are designed to make you think, and there is space for journaling and reflection. All that you need is here. So if you want to use these guides on your own, enjoy!

At the same time, these guides are especially designed for group discussion. (A group is two or more people, so you can have a great discussion even if you are with only one other person.)

Most of us grow in life and in our spirituality as we talk and share with others. People learn best in an active mode of participation, conversation and dialogue! And we gain so much by hearing the ideas and insights of others.

If you use these guides in a group discussion format, you will need a leader. The leader will spend extra time preparing in order to help everyone get the most out of the discussion. The leader's role is not to have all the answers. Instead, the leader helps facilitate the discussion, so that everyone learns from one another and from the wisdom in the guide and in the Bible.

The leader can best help the group by using the leader's notes that are included at the end of this guide.

How to Have a Great Discussion

Here are some suggestions that will make your discussion more helpful and more fun.

1. Read over the session beforehand. If everyone gets a chance to look over the theme and some of the questions and ideas, discussion will be more rich and stimulating.
2. Remind each other of some simple guidelines that can really help the discussion go well:
    - **a.** Have fun.
    - **b.** Ask questions. Any question that is a real question for someone is a *great* question.
    - **c.** Listen to each other, and build each other up. Affirm each other whenever you

feel genuine appreciation for an idea or insight.

d. Be open to spiritual growth.

e. Try to find answers from the Scripture passage when you are in that part of the discussion session. If people start going on lots of tangents, you may never get anywhere!

f. Help each other contribute but not dominate. Everyone has something to say, but no one has it all!

3. If a particular question interests you, then do some further reading and discussion with others between meetings.

The Format of Each Session

Each overall session is oriented around a question that seekers and skeptics have often asked. The introduction opens up ways different people in our culture might respond to the key question. "Going Deeper" helps us get "underneath" to uncover the real questions we have. "User's Guide" orients us to the Bible wisdom we will discuss. "The Oracle" is a Bible passage that addresses the topic. "Musing" has questions for group discussion around the Scripture and the overall theme. "Challenge" summarizes the wisdom in the Bible section and suggests what choices we may face. "God Moment" describes how someone has found freedom and personal growth. "Self-Reflection" gives you a chance to reflect on and perhaps journal about your own journey. There may also be an optional prayer you can use as you feel comfortable.

About This Series

Spiritual hunger is at an all-time high. But people are not necessarily interested in traditional ways of meeting that hunger. So some leaders from InterVarsity Christian Fellowship and Willow Creek Community Church's Axis Ministry have created these guides as an answer to people who are spiritually interested but looking for fresh ways to explore their interest.

We are seeing an exploding movement of "Groups Investigating God"—people meeting together to have discussions like these. We hope you will benefit from these discussions as you find your way in life.

At the end of the guide, we give you other resources and help for your journey.

Rick Richardson

Series Editor

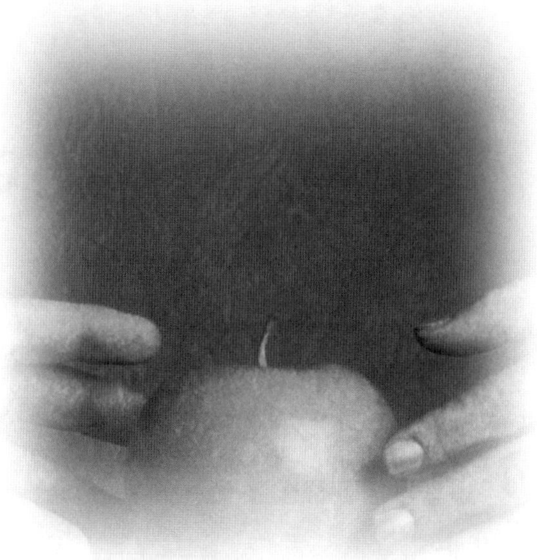

ONE
IS GOD AGAINST SEX & PLEASURE?

SALLY: They had these days of the week underpants, and I thought they were sort of funny. And then one day my boyfriend says to me, "You never wear Sunday." He's all suspicious. Where was Sunday? Where did I leave Sunday? And I told him, and he didn't believe me.

HARRY: What?

SALLY: They don't make Sunday.

HARRY: Why not?

SALLY: Because of God.

WHEN HARRY MET SALLY

Rick's story: When I first considered Christian faith, one of my strong objections was that Christians seemed so uptight about sex and pleasure. They seemed to alternate between guilt and repression, almost like they were still living in the sexually obsessed but straight-laced Victorian era. I wasn't sure why they were so hung up, but I knew that I didn't want to join them. I liked sexual experiences and thought people ought to be free to express that part of themselves, as long as they respected other people's needs and wishes. If two people liked each other, heterosexually or homosexually, what business was it of mine, or of anybody else, what they did to express their affection and to experience pleasure? If God was against sex and pleasure, and just made people feel uptight and guilty about natural desires and experiences, then I didn't want anything to do with that kind of God.

■ ***Do you feel that way too? Why or why not?***

Going Deeper

Many of us grew up experiencing a form of Christianity that seemed to be against fun, sex and pleasure. We never heard people in the church talk about sex. It was a taboo subject.

Others of us would not ever go to a church because we would fear that all we would find there is judgment and condemnation for our sexual choices.

Neither of these approaches to sexuality is healthy. If sexual fulfillment and sexual integrity go together, and if both spirituality and sexuality are core to who we are, then we need to explore the links between our sexuality and our spirituality. In the process we will discover how God really views sex and pleasure.

User's Guide

Each week we will look at what the Bible really says about sex. We're not assuming you believe the Bible is the Word of God; we're just assuming that we will be helped by looking together at the wisdom for living that the Bible has to offer. We will begin with the first book of the Bible, Genesis.

The Oracle

Then the LORD God formed man from the dust of the ground, and breathed into his nostrils the breath of life; and the man became a living being. . . .

The LORD God took the man and put him in the garden of Eden to till it and keep it. And the LORD God commanded the man, "You may freely eat of every tree of the garden; but of the tree of the knowledge of good and evil you shall not eat, for in the day that you eat of it you shall die."

Then the LORD God said, "It is not good that the man should be alone; I will make him a helper as his partner." So out of the ground, the LORD God formed every animal of the field and every bird of the air, and brought them to the man to see what he would call them; and whatever the man called every living creature, that was its name. The man gave names to all cattle, and to the birds of the air, and to every animal of the field; but for the man there was not found a helper as his partner. So the LORD God caused a deep sleep to fall upon the man, and he slept; then he took one of his ribs and closed up its place with flesh. And the rib that the LORD God had taken from the man he made into a woman and brought her to the man. Then the man said,

"This at last is bone of my bones
    and flesh of my flesh;
this one shall be called Woman,
    for out of Man this one was taken."

Therefore a man leaves his father and his mother and clings to his wife, and they become one flesh. And the man and his wife were both naked, and were not ashamed. (Genesis 2:7, 15-25)

Musing

1. What is most striking to you in this account of the creation of human beings?
2. Do you think this account is meant to be strictly historical, or do you think it's more meant to give us insight into what it means to be human? Explain.
3. Right away, we are told that we are both physical and spiritual. We are made from the dust of the earth (our physical side) and the breath of God (our spiritual side). Do you think these two sides of our humanity, physical and spiritual, are more in conflict with each other or more in harmony with each other, and why?

4. God also gives them a boundary—not to eat any fruit except the fruit of the tree of the knowledge of good and evil. Why do you think God gives them this particular boundary? (Hint: "Eating the fruit" implies knowing the consequences of both good and evil by direct personal experience.)
5. The passage tells us it's not good for a man to be alone. What does the man think of God's final solution?
6. The passage then says that the man and the woman become "one flesh." What do you think that might mean?
7. According to these verses, sex seems to involve the union of both parts of who we are, physical and spiritual. It is much more than just pleasure. How do you respond to this idea?
8. If in sex we become one with others physically and spiritually, what limits and boundaries to sexual union might this passage imply?
9. From this passage, how would you answer the question we started with: Is God against sex and pleasure? Explain your response.

Challenge

God made us as sexual beings. Sex can bring great joy and wholeness to our lives. But sex is very powerful. It is not just a physical act, but also an emotional and even spiritual act. Sex can be like a powerful coursing river. When it escapes its banks, its right boundaries, it can cause much chaos and damage in our lives. Within the right limits, sex is a wonderful, good, important gift for us. We not only ought to feel comfortable with our own bodies and our own sexuality, we also ought to celebrate those things about us.

■ ***Talk about whether you agree or disagree with this challenge and why.***

■ ***Why do you think that, in a society that seems to celebrate the physical body so much, most of us have such a poor body image?***

GOD MOMENT

Rick's Story, Part Two

In college, I had a series of relationships with women. I felt like I didn't really know who I was, nor did I have a sense of contentment or well-being unless I was in a dating relationship. I would leave a relationship or be left, and within weeks, and sometimes even before the old relationship fell apart, I would be in another relationship. Sexual experiences were an important part of those relationships.

As I began to seek God in college, I realized I was trying to fill an emptiness inside that was often being made worse by all these relationships and sexual experiences. In the end, I was not less lonely but more lonely. I found that sometimes the sex part covered over the lack of real friendship and compatibility in some of my relationships. And I also found that having sex in a relationship made breaking up later all the more painful. So I started to ask God to fill that emptiness and loneliness so my relationships would work better and bring healing, not more hurt. I will never forget the night I decided to commit my life to seeking God and God's way for my relationships and my sex life. It was not an easy choice for me at all. But looking back, it has made all the difference.

■ ***Can you relate to Rick's story? How?***

Self-Reflection

This is a place for you to journal your thoughts and ideas.

What in this study do you want to reflect on further?

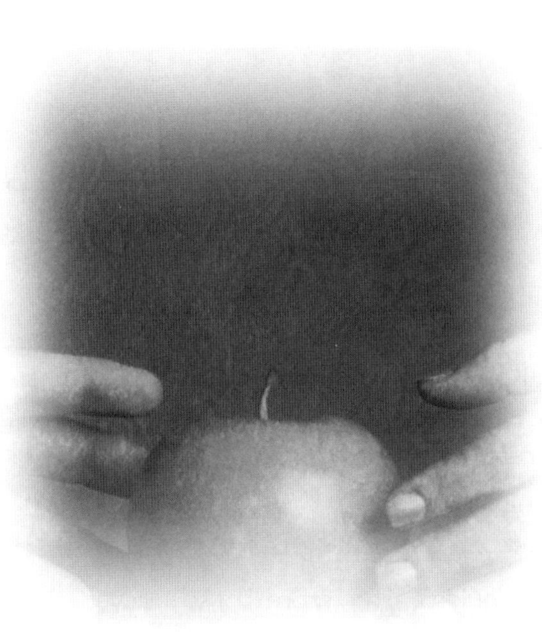

15

TWO
IS THERE HELP FOR SEXUAL MISTAKES & REGRETS?

SALLY: It [sex] was a mistake!

HARRY: I'm so relieved you think so. I'm not saying last night wasn't great. It was.

SALLY: Yes it was.

HARRY: We just never should have done it.

SALLY: I couldn't agree more. I'm so relieved.

WHEN HARRY MET SALLY

Melissa's story: I had been going out with Ted for about a month when I started feeling the pressure from him to have sex. I wasn't ready. But I didn't want him to leave me either. I really liked the guy. But I sensed that he expected me to go to bed with him and would be very disappointed, maybe not even stick around, if I didn't go along. About a week later, I did sleep with him. I was so disappointed. I didn't really feel that he cared for me in the experience, and I couldn't even look at him the next day. It was a mistake and one of my biggest regrets. It wasn't that

I felt sex was wrong. It's just it wasn't special like I'd always thought. I've had sex since, but I do it on my own terms a little more. And I've realized that guys who won't stick with me unless I give out are probably not worth keeping.

■ ***How do you respond to Melissa's story?***

Going Deeper

We've probably all done things we regret in the sexual side of our lives. Maybe we were like Melissa and had sex out of feeling pressured and not out of choice. Maybe we've slept with someone and it was a betrayal of someone else. Maybe we've gotten involved in private sexual images or experiences where we've felt out of control or ashamed.

Where do we go with the shame? How do we deal with past mistakes and regrets so that they don't undermine our sexual integrity and fulfillment in the future?

User's Guide 17

Here is Jesus' wisdom on how to deal with mistakes and regrets. He was speaking to the Pharisees, who were the teachers of Jewish law. In the setting described here they would have been reclining sideways on the floor around a low table.

The Oracle

> One of the Pharisees asked Jesus to eat with him, and he went into the Pharisee's house and took his place at the table. And a woman in the city, who was a sinner, having learned that he was eating in the Pharisee's house, brought an alabaster jar of ointment. She stood behind him at his feet weeping, and began to bathe his feet with her tears and to dry them with her hair. Then she continued kissing his feet and anointing them with the ointment. Now when the Pharisee who had invited him saw this, he said to himself, "If this man were a prophet, he would have known who and what kind of woman this is who is touching him—that she is a sinner." Jesus spoke up and said to him, "Simon, I have something to say to you." "Teacher," he replied, "Speak." "A certain creditor had two debtors; one owed five hundred denarii [about $24,000 in today's terms], and the other fifty [$2,400]. When they could not pay, he canceled the debts for both of them. Now which of them will love him more?" Simon

answered, "I suppose the one for whom he canceled the greater debt." And Jesus said to him, "You have judged rightly." Then turning to the woman, he said to Simon, "Do you see this woman? I entered your house; you gave me no water for my feet, but she has bathed my feet with her tears and dried them with her hair. You gave me no kiss, but from the time I came in she has not stopped kissing my feet. You did not anoint my head with oil, but she has anointed my feet with ointment. Therefore, I tell you, her sins, which were many, have been forgiven; hence she has shown great love. But the one to whom little is forgiven, loves little." Then he said to her, "Your sins are forgiven." But those who were at the table with him began to say among themselves, "Who is this who even forgives sins?" And he said to the woman, "Your faith has saved you; go in peace." (Luke 7:36-50)

Musing

1. Imagine that you are at this dinner party. This woman was probably a prostitute, and "decent people" would have despised her. What strikes you about what she does?
2. Why do you think she acts like this?
3. Pharisees are like the perfectionistic, self-righteous people we know. Do you know anyone who is like this host, and if so, how do you feel around this person?
4. What does this woman's response to Jesus suggest to you about what Jesus and God are like?
5. Is that how you see or think about God, and why or why not?
6. What do you think Jesus means when he tells the woman that her sins are forgiven and her faith has saved her? (How can faith save a person?)
7. At this point, how important would you say it is to you to become closer to God (like this woman was)?
8. I John 1:9 says, "If we confess our sins, he who is faithful and just will forgive us our sins and cleanse us from all unrighteousness." How might this teaching help us with past sexual mistakes and regrets?

Challenge

Jesus (and God) are loving and accepting and forgiving toward people that have really messed up—when they know they have messed up and come to God to be cleansed and forgiven. Those people have a very special closeness to God because they know how much God has forgiven them. Self-righteous people, who think they have no sexual problems or failures, can be apathetic toward God, not really thinking they need anything from God.

When we know we're accepted and forgiven, we are free to really be close to God. Do you want that kind of closeness?

■ ***How do you respond?***

GOD MOMENT

Melissa's Story, Part Two

After I started a relationship with God, I was glad I could admit my mistake and take my regrets about Ted to God. I felt cleansed and forgiven by God. But the biggest surprise to me was that I started to respect myself more. I look back on that time with Ted, and I know he wasn't worth it. I want so much more from sexual involvement than I wanted at that point in my life. I want sex to be good for my soul.

Self-Reflection

What do you do with sexual mistakes and regrets?

What might help you grow in self respect and move toward greater sexual integrity?

IS THERE HEALING FOR SEXUAL HURTS?

> Hi. It's me. It's the holiday season, and I thought I'd remind you that it's the season of charity and forgiveness. And although it is not widely known, it is also the season of groveling. So if you feel like calling me back, I'd be more than happy to do the traditional Christmas grovel. Call me.
>
> (HARRY'S APOLOGY TO SALLY AFTER THEY SLEEP TOGETHER AND THEN DECIDE IT WAS A MISTAKE)
> ***WHEN HARRY MET SALLY***

Janet's story: When I was in college, I worked at a restaurant as a waitress. After work sometimes, all of us who worked there would hang out. One New Year's Eve, I went to the home of one of the managers. I thought I was attending a party that all my coworkers were also attending. When I got to my manager's house, I was surprised that I was the first one there. He asked me in, took my coat and went back to the door. Then he locked it. That began for me a nightmare evening that has marked my life. My boss raped me that night. Even worse, a couple of the people who I thought were my friends had helped him set it up. I felt so betrayed. But I also felt dirty and guilty, like somehow it had been my fault, like somehow I had deserved what had happened.

After that night I took a long vacation from God, from relationships, from trusting anyone or anybody. I built a wall. And it was years before I had any desire to be with a man, or to be intimate, emotionally or physically. I became convinced that I could never really trust anybody ever again.

■ ***Have you ever wondered where God was when you had some hurtful experience? Or have you ever blamed yourself for something that wasn't really your fault? If you can, talk about your thoughts and feelings toward God or yourself as you've gone through tough times.***

Going Deeper

What evil there is in the world! Too many women have experienced abuse or rape. Men too have been hurt, by older men or by insensitive women. And both men and women go through painful breakups of relationships they wanted to keep.

Sexual hurts and wounds go to the core of who we are. We need to find healing for those hurts if we are to achieve sexual integrity and fulfillment. Unless they are healed, such wounds can stay with us and undermine our sexual relationships for the rest of our lives.

User's Guide

Each week we are looking at the wisdom of Jesus for the question we're asking. This week we will look at a woman who had sought healing for years and had not been able to get help. For her, the wound was not related to past sexual involvement, but it did go to the core of who she was as a woman in her sexuality.

The Oracle

> A large crowd followed him and pressed in on him. Now there was a woman who had been suffering from hemorrhages for twelve years. She had endured much under many physicians, and had spent all that she had; and she was no better, but rather grew worse. She had heard about Jesus, and came up behind him in the crowd and touched his cloak, for she said, "If I but touch his clothes, I will be made well." Immediately her hemorrhage stopped; and she felt in her body that she was healed of her disease. Immediately aware that power had gone forth from him, Jesus turned about in the crowd and said, "Who touched my clothes?" And his disciples said to

him, "You see the crowd pressing in on you; how can you say, 'Who touched me?'" He looked all around to see who had done it. But the woman, knowing what had happened to her, came in fear and trembling, fell down before him, and told him the whole truth. He said to her, "Daughter, your faith has made you well; go in peace, and be healed of your disease." (Mark 5:24-34)

Musing

1. In her culture, this woman, who had had her period nonstop for twelve years, would have been considered unclean, not able to marry, with a stigma attached to her reputation. What kinds of things in our culture carry a stigma, even though the person may or may not have done anything wrong?
2. The woman tried everything to end her suffering and get rid of the stigma, but with no success. What are the ways people today can try to solve their suffering and get rid of their feelings of shame?
   Do you think these solutions work or not, and why?

3. The woman was convinced that Jesus could help her and heal her. Why might she have felt that way?
4. She touched his robe, was healed and then ran away. Why might Jesus have sought her out and made her go public?
5. How might Jesus' very positive words to the woman have helped her, in her self-image and in her reputation with others?
6. Do you know anyone who is (even a little) like Jesus in how they affirm people and offer dignity? If so, describe that person.
7. What might Jesus say to people today who are feeling unworthy and like they have a stigma attached to them?

Challenge

Jesus loves to free people from shame. Jesus' followers didn't get it. Why was Jesus asking who touched him in that crowd? Sometimes, Jesus' followers don't get it today either. They don't understand how healing Jesus can be for people locked in shame or poor self-image.

But if you will talk to Jesus, ask him what he wants to say to you and listen, you might be very surprised at what Jesus wants to say. Jesus specializes in releasing people from shame and in restoring their self-respect, their sense of being loved and lovable.

■ ***How do you respond?***

GOD MOMENT

Janet's Story, Part Two

I became a part of a church in the city a few years later. This church really met the needs of people, and it was a very healing place. At one point in my time there, I was finally able to ask Jesus back into the center of my life. One concrete way I did that was that I invited Jesus to enter the image I had of those moments with my coworker. Jesus came into that picture in a very real way, touched me, lifted the shame and the fear I had felt, and showed me he would heal my hurting heart. I felt Jesus' presence at that moment in a profound way. As much as the nightmare of that night years ago has affected my life, the experience of the tangible presence of Jesus has affected my life even more. I felt like I got a fresh start. Finally, I found myself wanting to be intimate with a man, wanting a husband. I hadn't experienced those feelings in years.

Self-Reflection

Where do you need to be healed on the inside from shame or a sense of low self worth?

What might Jesus be saying to you, and how will you respond?

FOUR

IS THERE HOPE FOR SEXUAL STRUGGLES?

Men and women can't be friends because the sex part always gets in the way.

(HARRY)
WHEN HARRY MET SALLY

Jay's story: I realize it started for me in my early years, when I always felt criticized and distant from my mom. As I entered college, I gradually increased my involvement with porn. It numbed my inner anxiety, even though I felt humiliated and dirty afterward. Over time, those feelings of shame gradually disappeared. In college, porn, freaking and fake orgasm competitions helped dull any sense that I was doing anything wrong.

After college, I got married. I looked at marriage as my last hope for a solution to my inner emptiness and destructive involvement with pornography. But my wife could never measure up to that air-brushed perfection of magazines and videos. Soon I was visiting clubs and then began to have sex outside my marriage. I spent a lot of money, and I had to lie to keep my expenditures and my extracurricular activities secret from my wife.

One day, when my wife was home, and I didn't know it, I called one of those phone numbers for phone sex. She heard some of it. That day my marriage began to unravel. And I wasn't even sure I cared.

■ ***Why do you think people might get into pornography and other non-relational expressions of sexuality?***

Going Deeper

We all struggle at some level in our sexual relationships. For some of us, it was a traumatic breakup with a person we were sexually involved with. The pain has left us unable to trust others much. For others it's more related to the unique struggles common to our gender.

For women, sex and emotional involvement seem to go together more. Women may find themselves in dependent or enmeshed relationships that undermine self-respect and blur appropriate boundaries. Women may also choose to trade sex in order to keep a guy around.

Men are more visual and can be less connected up inside. Men seem more able to detach their emotions and their relational commitments from sex. As a result, men can become addicted to pornography and detached in their sexual relationships. But in the long run, that detachment will undermine any meaningful sexual experience or relationship.

When women have been rejected by absent or hurtful fathers, and when men have been rejected by controlling or distant mothers, relational and sexual addictions are common.

How do we find the strength and perspective to move toward sexual wholeness? How do we overcome addictive or destructive patterns in our lives?

■ ***How do you respond to this description of the tendencies of men and women in relation to sex and relationships?***

User's Guide

We'll be focusing on some words from the most famous teaching Jesus ever gave, the Sermon on the Mount. Jesus had looked around at his culture and at the religious people of his day, and he realized that they didn't really get the point of religion and faith. So he taught people a new way, a way of radical love for God and others.

The final paragraph was written by the apostle Paul.

Oracle

You have heard that it was said, "You shall not commit adultery." But I say to you that everyone who looks at a woman with lust has already committed adultery with her in his heart. If your right eye causes you to sin, tear it out and throw it away; it is better for you to lose one of your members than for your whole body to be thrown into hell. And if your right hand causes you to sin, cut it off and throw it away; it is better for you to lose one of your members than for your whole body to go into hell. It was also said, "Whoever divorces his wife, let him give her a certificate of divorce." But I say to you that anyone who divorces his wife, except on the ground of unchastity, causes her to commit adultery; and whoever marries a divorced woman commits adultery. (Matthew 5:27-32)

Do not judge, so that you may not be judged. For with the judgment you make you will be judged, and the measure you give will be the measure you get. . . .

Ask, and it will be given to you; search, and you will find; knock, and the door will be opened for you. For everyone who asks receives, and for everyone who searches finds, and for everyone who knocks, the door will be opened. Is there anyone among you who, if your child asks for bread, will give him a stone? Or if the child asks for a fish, will give a snake? If you then, who are evil, know how to give good gifts to your children, how much more will your Father in heaven give good gifts to those who ask him! (Matthew 7:1-2, 7-11)

No testing has overtaken you that is not common to everyone. God is faithful, and he will not let you be tested beyond your strength, but with the testing he will also provide the way out so that you may be able to endure it. (1 Corinthians 10:13)

Musing

1. People in Jesus' day made a big deal of adultery but thought lust was fine. How would you define *lust?*
2. Do you think lust is destructive, and, if so, when?

3. Jesus has very severe advice for how we should deal with lust in our lives. What do you think Jesus is saying, and how do you feel about his advice?

4. Jesus tells us not to judge others. Is he contradicting himself when he is so severe about lust and yet so clear about being nonjudgmental and loving, and why or why not?

5. Then Jesus tells us to pray and ask God for good gifts. How does Jesus make the point that we can expect God to answer our prayers?

6. Look again at the final paragraph. What does Paul tell us we can expect from God when we experience sexual temptation, addiction or struggle?

7. In light of the promise that Paul gives about temptation and that Jesus gives about prayer, how might you want to pray to God about areas of sexual struggle?

Challenge

God is good! God is powerful! God loves to give good gifts to people who ask.

Do you have a struggle in the area of your sexuality? God wants you to ask for help. God is a forgiver, a leader and a healer in our lives. If we will commit to going God's way, God will commit to giving us perspective and strengthening us to live in new ways. We can get a fresh start. We can get help, even in areas of relational and sexual addiction.

God is good! God is powerful!

■ ***How do you respond?***

GOD MOMENT

Jay's Story, Part Two

After I lost my marriage, I ended up more and more lonely. Finally, I decided to seek out help. A church I had visited had a ministry called Restoration for men with sexual addictions. The toughest part for me was admitting that I had a sexual addiction, even though it was so obvious to others. But when I did, and I began to attend the meetings, I found other people who struggled similarly and who were getting help from God and each other. That decision became a turning point in my life. Please, if you're reading this, and you have sexually or emotionally dependent or addictive tendencies, don't wait as long as I did to get help. It cost me a lot to wait so long and made getting back so much harder.

Self-Reflection

Where do you want to ask for the help of God and others in your life?

How might you need to begin to go God's way in your sexual choices?

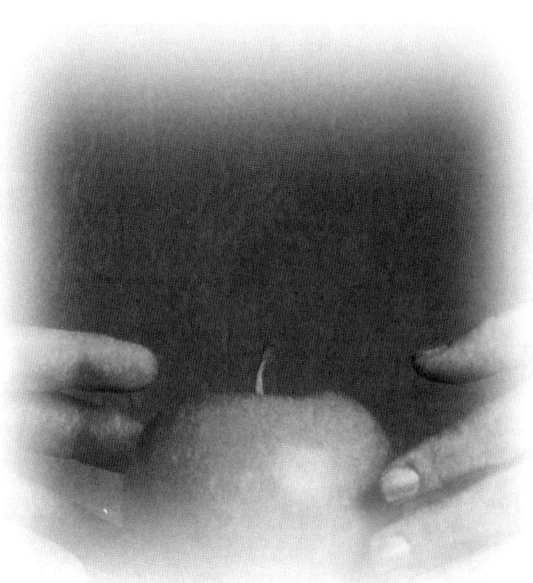

29

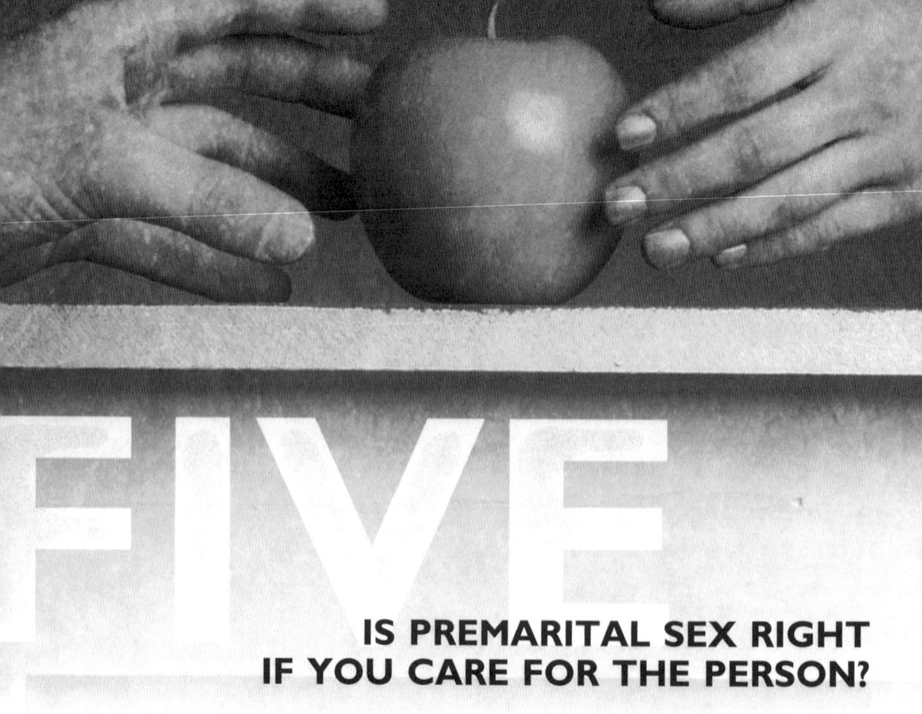

FIVE

IS PREMARITAL SEX RIGHT IF YOU CARE FOR THE PERSON?

SALLY: You want to act like what happened [sex] didn't mean anything.

HARRY: I'm not saying it didn't mean anything. I'm saying why does it have to mean everything?

SALLY: Because it does. And you should know that better than anybody, because the minute that it does, you walk right out the door.

HARRY: I didn't walk out.

SALLY: No, sprinted is more like it.

WHEN HARRY MET SALLY

Jim's story: I met Lisa in the summer after my senior year in high school. I think she liked me right away, but in the beginning I just wanted to be friends. In the fall, we went off to college to different schools. But my school was in her hometown, so we kept seeing each other. In October of that fall, I went to the beach with her family along the New Jersey shore. Lisa and I stayed up all night talking and watched the sun rise together the next morning. That afternoon, we began to be physical with each other. That weekend, I started to fall in love.

Over the next few months, we kept seeing each other. We could talk forever, it seemed, and we shared our thoughts and dreams and struggles with each other. We had our favorite restaurant (Chinese), our favorite picnic spot (a wooded area near where Lisa went to school) and our favorite thing to do (make out!). Near Christmas, we slept together for the first time. I felt so in love. I know she did too. She even told her mom the next day. Her mom smiled at me when she saw me. "You got your Christmas present early, didn't you?"

I had grown up in a family that wasn't very close. The relationship with Lisa came to mean so much to me. We cared for each other, and we both wanted to be connected in every way possible.

It all felt so right. What could be wrong with that?

■ ***Do you agree with Jim that if people care for each other and it feels right, sleeping together is fine? Why or why not?***

Going Deeper

We live in a very feeling-oriented culture. If it feels right, go for it. Just do it. It is very difficult to even begin to question that basic orientation of our society.

But we have to ask the hard questions about sex if we are to discover and achieve true sexual integrity and fulfillment. If we are to connect up body and soul, relational commitments and sexual experiences, we have to look at premarital and extramarital sex. What does intercourse bring about between people? How do we keep our integrity and our sense of self-worth high over the long run in the ways we make sexual choices and commitments? Are there unintended consequences of sex outside marriage that we need to know about?

User's Guide

Jesus' words about sex in Matthew 19:4-6 were that at the beginning the Creator "'made them male and female. . . . For this reason a man shall leave his father and mother and be joined to his wife, and the two shall become one flesh.' So they are no longer two, but one." One of Jesus' early followers, Paul, applied Jesus' ideas in

I Corinthians 6. This passage is hard-hitting and direct.

The Oracle

> "All things are lawful for me," but not all things are beneficial. "All things are lawful for me," but I will not be dominated by anything. "Food is meant for the stomach and the stomach for food," and God will destroy both one and the other. The body is meant not for fornication [sexual oneness outside of marriage] but for the Lord, and the Lord for the body. And God raised the Lord and will also raise us by his power. Do you not know that your bodies are members of Christ? Should I therefore take the members of Christ and make them members of a prostitute? Never! Do you not know that whoever is united to a prostitute becomes one body with her? For it is said, "The two shall be one flesh." But anyone united to the Lord becomes one spirit with him. Shun fornication! Every sin that a person commits is outside the body; but the fornicator sins against the body itself. Or do you not know that your body is a temple of the Holy Spirit within you, which you have from God, and that you are not your own? For you were bought with a price; therefore glorify God in your body.
> (I Corinthians 6:12-20)

Musing

1. Paul starts talking not about boundaries but about true freedom in verses 12-13. What do you think he is saying?
2. Paul talks about food and sex becoming dominant in the lives of the people of his time, running and ruining their lives. What parts do food and sex addictions have in our culture and in people today?
3. Paul talks about sex as a body- and life-uniting act. What do you think it is about sex that makes it so bonding for our bodies and our souls?
4. Why might it be contradictory to be one with a prostitute and also one with God?
5. What do you think Paul might mean when he says that sexual sin is unlike other sin: it is a sin against the body?
6. What do you think might be the negative consequences of sex outside of marriage?

7. What difference might it make to the way you live if you really thought of your body as God's home?

Challenge

God wants to make his home in us. He wants to be one with us.

In sex, people become one. Their bodies and their souls mingle. We trivialize sex when we believe it is only about pleasure. It is also about intimacy and commitment. When we become one with people and mingle our souls and bodies with theirs, there are consequences. When we do that for pleasure, outside of commitment and intimacy and oneness, we become less whole, more fragmented as people. We give away parts of ourselves that we were meant to give away much more carefully.

Even when we have sex with others that we feel love for, there is still great pain when we break up.

Being sex mates and being soul mates were meant to go together; sex is best when there is trust and a lifelong commitment of marriage. We have an opportunity to use the gift of sex God's way. And invite God to make a home in us.

■ ***How do you respond to the soul challenge? Do you agree, disagree or not really care one way or the other?***

GOD MOMENT

Jim's Story, Part Two

My sophomore year in college, the inevitable happened. I went over to Lisa's home one cold February evening to tell her that I felt like the relationship needed to end. It was one of the hardest things I have ever had to do.

She was so hurt. She had been sure that our relationship was moving toward marriage. She had also had a time of doubt several months earlier, and I had convinced her to hang in. So she was also furious that she had listened and not broken up with me first. And her dad was absolutely furious that I had slept with his daughter and was now breaking up with her.

I still think about that relationship often. I gave a part of my soul away. I know I did.

I still feel badly about what happened to Lisa. People later told me the hurt had changed her personality some. She was no longer so trusting or warm. She also gave a part of her soul away. I wonder if she ever got it back.

Later, when I asked God to make a home in me, I was still involved sexually with another woman. I didn't want to give that up. But I knew I faced a fork in the road. Would I go God's way with sex, or would I go my own way? When I committed to going God's way, I had such a deep sense of God's presence and healing in my soul. That moment was one of the most important of my life. I gave up premarital sex. But I gained the sense of God's presence, peace and pleasure in my life. Ultimately, I laid the foundation for becoming much more whole as a person and much more happy with the place of sex in my life.

■ ***How do you respond to Jim's story?***

Self-Reflection

Take an honest look at the costs and benefits of going God's way with sexual relationships. What would it cost you to go God's way in your sexual choices? What would you gain? Which comes out ahead for you at this point in your life? What will you do about it?

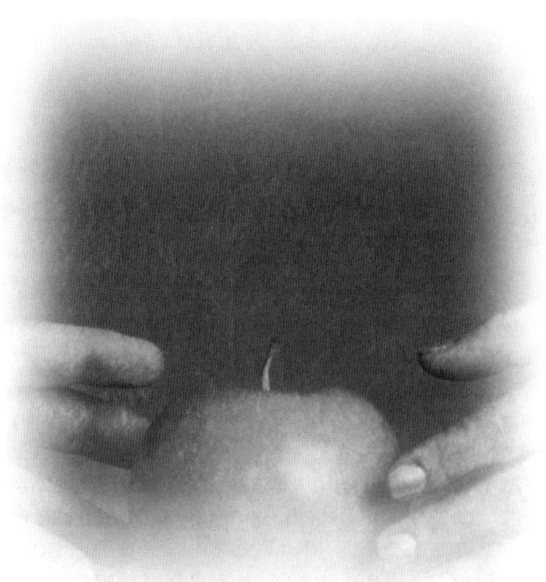

SIX

HOW DO I FIND SEXUAL INTEGRITY & FULFILLMENT?

HARRY: I love that you get cold when it's 71 degrees out. I love that it takes an hour and a half for you to order a sandwich. I love that you get a little crinkle above your nose when you look at me like I'm nuts. I love that when I spend a day with you I can still smell your perfume on my clothes. And I love that you are the last person I want to talk to before I go to sleep at night. And it's not because I'm lonely, and it's not because it's New Year's Eve. I came here tonight because when you realize you want to spend the rest of your life with somebody, you want the rest of your life to start as soon as possible.

SALLY: You see? That is just like you Harry. You say things like that, and you make it impossible to hate you. And I hate you, Harry. I really hate you.

(Then they kiss.)

WHEN HARRY MET SALLY

Diane's story: I met Ron at work. Frankly, I wasn't too happy in my marriage. My husband was a good dad, but we very rarely connected. All the romantic voltage we had had while dating had dwindled to almost nothing by then. I needed to feel like I was in love again. I needed to feel like I was attractive again. I needed to be paid attention to and romanced again.

Ron was so attentive, and we connected. So over a few months, I decided to take the plunge. One night, we both stayed after work and talked. Talking turned to touching. A lingering hug goodbye turned into a kiss. The next week we arranged to sleep together.

After the affair began, I felt so alive at first. But I also felt worried about how my husband would respond if he ever found out. In the end, he did, and our marriage ended. I guess I felt the worst about the kids.

■ ***Why do you think the incidences of adultery and sex outside of marriage are so high?***

Going Deeper

There is a firm called Alibi Agency whose sole purpose is to furnish plausible lies and corroborating evidence for sexually unfaithful spouses. They have received ten thousand customer inquiries this year, and they plan to open other franchises in multiple countries. Their advertisement: "We want to protect your loved ones from the stress that goes with suspecting a spouse is unfaithful." It should come as no surprise that adultery is at an all-time high in the United States.

Many people afraid of divorce and wanting to test drive their sexual and relational compatibility before marriage choose to live together. But the test drive theory doesn't seem to work. For instance, the *Houston Chronicle* reports that couples who live together before marriage have an 80 percent higher likelihood of getting divorced than couples that don't live together before marriage. And the collateral damage of breakups for those who don't ever get married is high as well.

Maybe our sexual needs won't really be fulfilled until we also fulfill the spiritual longings we have. At least that's what Jesus seems to say to a woman he met who was very sexually active and confused, but also spiritually seeking and open.

User's Guide

We will look at an encounter Jesus had with a woman in Samaria, a country just

North of Jerusalem. The Jews hated Samaria and Samaritans. They were half-breeds, mixed-blood Jews, the people from the other side of the tracks. Not surprisingly for Jesus, he was again making big trouble for himself with religious-type people by hanging out with despised minority women and risking charges of scandal.

The woman was out at midday at a time when respectable women in the Middle East were inside. She had a checkered past. But Jesus picked her out as a likely candidate for a relationship with God. Her sexual search apparently pointed to a deeper spiritual search.

For your reference, Jacob and Joseph were key father figures in founding Israel centuries before Jesus.

The Oracle

Now when Jesus learned that the Pharisees had heard, "Jesus is making and baptizing more disciples than John"—although it was not Jesus himself but his disciples who baptized—he left Judea and started back to Galilee. But he had to go through Samaria. So he came to a Samarian city called Sychar, near the plot of ground Jacob had given to his son Joseph. Jacob's well was there, and Jesus, tired out by his journey, was sitting by the well. It was about noon.

A Samaritan woman came to draw water, and Jesus said to her, "Give me a drink." (His disciples had gone to the city to buy food.) The Samaritan woman said to him, "How is it that you, a Jew, ask a drink of me, a woman of Samaria?" (Jews do not share things in common with Samaritans.) Jesus answered her, "If you knew the gift of God, and who it is that is saying to you, 'Give me a drink,' you would have asked him and he would have given you living water." The woman said to him, "Sir, you have no bucket and the well is deep. Where do you get that living water? Are you greater than our ancestor Jacob, who gave us this well, and with his sons and his flocks drank from it?" Jesus said to her, "Everyone who drinks of this water will be thirsty again, but those who drink of the water that I will give them will never be thirsty. The water that I give will become in them a spring of water gushing up to eternal life." The woman said to him, "Sir, give me this water, so that I may never be thirsty or have to keep coming here to draw water."

Jesus said to her, "Go call your husband, and come back." The woman answered him, "I have no husband." Jesus said to her, "You are right in saying, 'I have no husband'; for you have had five husbands, and the one you have now is not your husband. What you have said is true!" The woman said to him, "Sir, I see that you are a prophet. Our ancestors worshiped on this mountain, but you say that the place where people should worship is in Jerusalem." Jesus said to her, "Woman, believe me, the hour is coming when you will worship the Father neither on this mountain nor in Jerusalem. You worship what you do not know; we worship what we know, for salvation is from the Jews. But the hour is coming, and is now here, when the true worshipers will worship the Father in spirit and truth, for the Father seeks such as these to worship him. God is spirit, and those who worship him must worship in spirit and truth." The woman said to him, "I know that Messiah is coming" (who is called Christ). "When he comes, he will proclaim all things to us." Jesus said to her, "I am he, the one who is speaking to you." . . .

Many Samaritans from that city believed in him because of the woman's testimony, "He told me everything I have ever done." (John 4:1-26, 39)

Musing

1. Jesus asks the woman for a drink. How does Jesus' request begin to break down the cultural and gender barriers of Jesus' day?
2. The woman can't get past the barriers, but Jesus ignores her question and offers her living water. What are the characteristics of the water Jesus offers?
3. What do you think Jesus is really offering when he talks about living water?
4. The woman asks for the living water, and so Jesus tells her to call her husband. What does Jesus know about the woman and her past, and how does that make the woman feel?
5. How would it feel to encounter someone who seemed to know the story of your life and the secrets of your heart without being told, and who still liked and respected you, like Jesus did with this woman?
6. The Jews believed that God could only be worshiped in Jerusalem at the temple. How does Jesus redefine worship for this woman, and what do you think he means?
7. The woman puts her faith in Jesus and goes out to tell everyone from her town about him. What do you think most influenced the woman to become a follower of Jesus?

8. Take a moment to think about what Jesus might say to you if you met him in the flesh during a time of need or loneliness in your life. Try to picture what your thoughts and feelings would be in the midst of that encounter. Feel free to share anything that strikes you.

Challenge

Often our sexual longings point to deeper spiritual longings, and some of the more sexually active people are also people who most long for a meaningful connection to God.

In sex, we express our desire to be close to someone. The sexual drive will find its right expression in our lives as we settle the deeper question of spiritual closeness and union with God. Achieving true sexual integrity and fulfillment begins at the core of who we are. It begins with a commitment to God at the center of our lives.

Jesus offers a relationship of knowing and being known, of loving and being loved. He wants to tell us everything we ever did and begin to put our lives and our loves in order. And he offers living water that can flow out in genuine and whole sexual expression, and that will also flow out into life forever with God at the center of our lives.

- ***How do you respond to these ideas?***

GOD MOMENT

Diane's Story, Part Two

In my next year at work, I met a guy who was a Christian. He reached out to me, and he had a winning way about him. I had always had a lot of questions about Christianity. Like, if God is there, why have so many people suffered, and why is there so much pain and evil in the world? How could a loving God send people to hell? Why do Christians seem so uptight and repressed about sex?

Bob had some good answers, and I really felt cared for by him. He shared with me how to have a relationship with God, and I began to be very intrigued by Jesus. But I knew there was something I would never want to give up. The relationship and sexual involvement with Ron was still very important to me. If asking God in to the center of my life meant I would have to stop sleeping with Ron, I wasn't interested.

Bob just kept drawing me in, and I began to sense God's presence at work in my life. My desire to know God was growing. Finally, one cold February evening, I put my life in God's hands. I knew I was going to have to talk with Ron. I did. It was the hardest thing I ever did. But we stopped sleeping together and later broke up. I decided that I would trust that God knew best about sex. After all, God made it. And I decided that I would trust God with my life, that God would do good in my life.

I am reaching out to my kids in new ways, and I have talked with my former husband and let him know how sorry I am.

That choice to commit to God and trust God was the biggest and most important and life-changing decision I've ever made. That costly choice has been the most healthy thing I ever did.

Self-Reflection

Have you asked God to come into the center of your life and be your forgiver, healer and leader? Do you want to? On the following page is a simple prayer that can help you make that commitment if you are ready.

Look at the line below, and reflect on where you are right now in your spiritual journey and what your next step is:

Skeptical — Apathetic — Curious — Actively Seeking — Feeling Connected — Following God

A Simple Prayer to Invite God into the Center of Your Life

Thank you, God, that you made me to know you and love you and to find love and belonging in a relationship with you at the center of my life.

I ADMIT that I have replaced you at the center with other things and people. Specifically, (in your own words, tell God what you have put before God in your life). I have hurt you and others, and I choose now to turn from those things at the center of my life and back to you, God.

I ACCEPT that on the cross Jesus took on himself my sin of putting other things before you, God, and that he took on my spiritual death. And I thank you that you loved me so much that you sent your son to live and die for me.

I now ASK you, Jesus, to come into the center of my life, and I COMMIT myself to you as my forgiver, healer and leader. Thank you that you will restore my relationship with yourself and others, and that you will now change me from the inside out! Thank you Jesus!

You can get a simple summary of the message of God's love for you and how you can respond in the booklet called *Circles of Belonging*. This booklet will also help you to know how to get started in the adventure of a relationship with God at the center of your life.

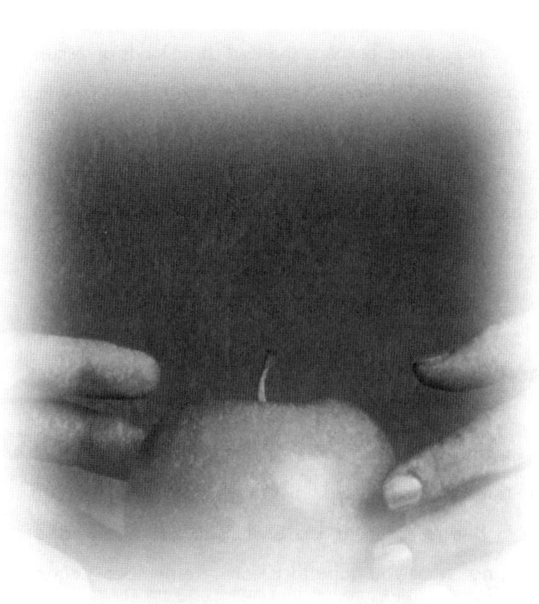

LEADING A GIG

You have decided to help others enter into investigating God. Welcome to a great adventure! The following notes will help you use this guide to facilitate excellent spiritual discussions with others.

The first step is inviting another person or persons to join you for these discussions. You can get a lot of help in this process by ordering *The GIG Guide*, a training guide that teaches you how to pray, invite, prepare and lead these kinds of discussions. You can get it from the books area of the InterVarsity Christian Fellowship webstore <www.ivcf.org/store> or by calling toll-free 1-866-265-4823.

Once you have found someone who wants to join you, you can begin preparing to lead the discussion. You don't need to be an expert or know lots about the Bible to lead the discussion. You only need to be willing to learn and grow yourself, and to serve others in their spiritual journey.

Getting Started

Here are some tips to help you lead the first discussion.

1. Be ready to share your excitement. As you prepare, think through why you are interested in this particular discussion and theme. Your excitement will help people enter in. But make sure to share what *you* personally hope to learn from the discussion, not what you hope *they* learn. Remember, your goal is not to "preach" your point of view but to facilitate a helpful discussion on important spiritual issues. I have found that when I have this kind of attitude, I leave a lot of room for others to find their own way and for God to work in all of our lives.
2. Think about how to make everyone feel comfortable. Find a convenient location for conversation. Arrange the seating so you can see everyone and they can see each other. Provide food and drinks if you wish. Buy guides for each potential participant so that they can follow along. You can ask them to pay you back if they want to keep the guide.
3. Make sure everyone has met each other. You might want to use an icebreaker

question to get people talking. You can find ideas at InterVarsity Press's Small Group Center: <www.ivpress.com/smallgroups/smallgroupidea>.

4. Read over the series introduction. In your first session, you will need to summarize what is in the guide. Put it in your own words, but try to stick to the ideas that are there. It is very important for people to get a sense that these discussions and conversations are for them and their search, and not just a chance for you to convince them of your point of view. So anything is fair game, any opinion is welcomed, and any question is good. Challenge them to make the discussion work for where they are at. And if something isn't helping, encourage them to speak up about it. Read the discussion guidelines in the series introduction. Those guidelines can be very helpful!
5. After you have summarized the overall purpose of the series, you can have the participants read the first part of the introduction that describes this particular guide. This orients everybody to the theme of the guide; it's more effective to read it than just summarize it. Be sensitive to slow readers. You may want to have someone (or yourself) read it aloud. It will help people feel more comfortable if you say something like, "We're reading the introduction just to get us all on the same page and to get us intrigued with what we'll be talking about." At the end, you can ask if people are intrigued.
6. Be aware of the discussion dynamics in your group. They will change depending on the number of people you have. If you have several people coming, your challenges will be helping everyone participate and making sure no one dominates. You can help people by affirming quieter people when they share and talking with dominant ones outside the group. Encourage dominant ones to join you in helping others express their opinions. If you have only one other person in your group, the dynamics are different. You will ask questions and then let the conversation go back and forth between you, sharing honestly. You become both a leader and a group participant at the same time! Either situation, we've found, can work very well.

How to Lead a Session

Prepare for each session by going through the discussion by yourself. Let it affect your life. Make notes on what is hitting you, what is helpful, how you are struggling, what questions you have and what difference the study is making in your life.

After you have gone through the study yourself, look again at the "Challenge." That segment provides the main point of the discussion. Write out in your own words summaries of the written sections that you will not be reading aloud during the discussion. Read through this study's section of the leader's notes. There you will find details about how each session will work.

You'll also find information in the leader's notes about how to cue your VCR for the video clips in the introductions. All the times given for the movie clips are for the videocassette version (VCR) that you can rent at any local video rental place. So the times include the previews. If you rent the DVD version, the times given in the guide will be a little high, because the DVD version doesn't include previews in the movie segment. Be sure the video is set at the right spot ahead of time.

In each session, you will need to choose which sections to read to the group and which to have the group read. Generally, you'll just want to have the group read a couple sections along with the Scripture passage. All other sections should be summarized by you or put in your own words. Otherwise the discussion may become too tied to the guide and be less dynamic.

1. *Introduction.* Some sessions begin with movie clips. This can be an engaging way to start the session and get the group's attention. Show the clip, and then ask the questions in that section. (You won't need to use the written introduction.) Remember, however, that the clips are simply meant to get people talking. Don't get sidetracked by overanalyzing the movie and its interpretation. It should not take you more than fifteen minutes to watch the clip and discuss the question.

If there is no clip, then you or another group member should read the introductory paragraphs aloud, and then you can ask the questions provided. This portion of the study is important in helping people open up to the topic. Some will be intimidated by the idea of Scripture study, and these general questions may help them begin to feel comfortable.

2. *Going Deeper.* Next summarize both the "Going Deeper" and the "User's Guide" sections.

3. *The Oracle.* It is generally most effective to have people read "The Oracle" section silently.

4. *Musing.* Depending on your experience and comfort level, you might use these questions as they are or put them in your own words. If you do reword them, be careful not to create "yes or no" questions; they will not foster discussion.

5. *Challenge.* After the discussion of the passage, summarize the challenge section, and ask for the group's response. The challenge is the main point of the study and should provide an overall focus for you as you prepare and lead.

6. *God Moment.* Allow a few moments of silence to have the group read "God Moment," or read it aloud if there is enough time left.

7. *Self-Reflection.* Summarize the "Self-Reflection" and simple prayer parts, and give the group a minute of quiet to think or to pray in their hearts if they want to. If you are studying one on one, then don't have a quiet reflection time, because it can feel awkward. Instead, summarize the "Self-Reflection" question and prayer, and ask if the person wants to respond.

Finally, end the discussion by introducing the theme for next time and telling people why you are excited about it.

Going Deeper

While you are encouraging others to talk, it is important for you to offer your own struggles and insights with honesty and vulnerability. Pick a couple of points during the study—once during the "Oracle" section and once during the "Challenge" or "God Moment" section—to speak about what you are learning and experiencing in your life.

Sometime after the fourth discussion and before the last one, take stock of yourself, and help others take stock of where they are at. It is helpful to meet one on one at that point. Use a tool like *Circles of Belonging* (InterVarsity Press) or another gospel outline to summarize the message of God's love, and ask how the person wants to respond to that message.

Contextualizing

The discussion dynamics and style that are most helpful for any group depend on the culture of the members of the group. We have found that the instructions for preparing and leading that we have given you above work well for many ethnically white, Asian and Native American groups. But be culturally sensitive. For Chinese Americans or Japanese Americans, a confrontational and highly personal approach might be uncomfortable.

African American, Latino American or Korean American participants, however, often appreciate a more passionate, direct and strongly led approach. In such a context, you probably would not want to read aloud any of the sections. This might seem insincere and artificial. Instead, you will want to summarize and passionately speak out your convictions and personal experiences all the way through, especially in the "Challenge" and "God Moment" sections.

Even if you are leading the group in a cultural context where you share more often and more passionately, make sure to include a couple of the "Musing" questions. Your aim is helping others with their journey. They will grow as they express their convictions and questions. And their answers will give you a good read on where they are coming from, so when you speak passionately you will be speaking to their situation.

So, on with the adventure! Have a blast.

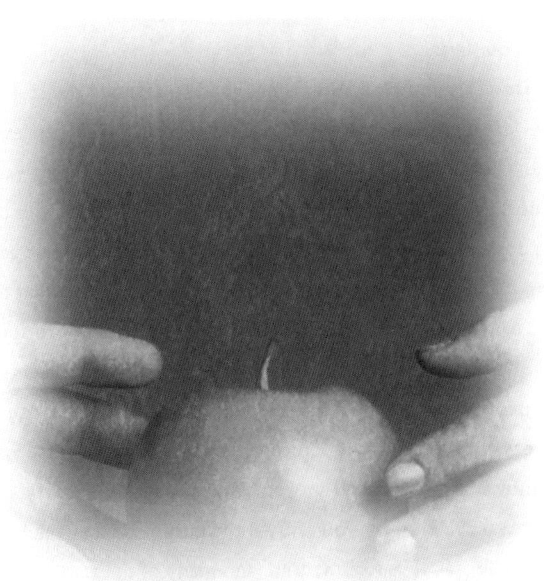

49

SESSION-BY-SESSION NOTES

Overall goal. To help people explore how to find sexual integrity and fulfillment by addressing questions about what God and sex have to do with each other:

Session One. Is God Against Sex & Pleasure?

Genesis 2:7, 15-25.

Main point. Sex is a gift of God that (within limits) can be immensely healing and wonderful in our lives.

General note. This first discussion is designed to explode the stereotypes that God and sex are opposites and that Christians are uptight and repressed when it comes to sex. Your challenge is to show how sex used in the right way is amazing, but misusing sex can be very destructive. So even though this study is focused on the positive, you will also need to look at the limits. Your goal is not to define the limits but to get the group thinking and talking about what they think the limits ought to be. Later discussions will explore the limits more specifically.

Video clip cue. The movie quotes in this guide are meant to be a fun way to introduce the question that will be discussed, but they are not intended to be for discussion in the way that they are in some of the other guides. In case your group really likes the movie clip approach, I am providing a cue for where the quote is in the movie. If you want to show it, you can. All the quotes come from *When Harry Met Sally.* That movie was very well-written, and many of the issues in the guide are also explored in the movie. The first quote comes at 9 minutes and 50 seconds into the video version of the movie.

Introduction. The personal stories at the beginning of each session in this guide play the same role as movie clips in other guides in the series. They introduce the question, establish personal connection and help create an environment in which people can express different opinions and feel accepted. So it is important to have people read these stories and respond. And it is important for you to affirm people in whatever way you can for what they express.

Question 2. The reason for asking this question is to let people express one barrier they may have to studying this passage. At this point, it doesn't matter whether or not they think the account is historical. Whatever they think about how historical the passage is, it certainly gives us some great wisdom and insight, and that's all we're looking for in this discussion.

Question 4. What God is against is our knowing the consequences of evil by direct personal experience. To eat the fruit of the tree of the knowledge of good and evil includes having the personal experience of evil. This participation in evil mars our humanity. Genesis 3, the next passage, gives the account of this participation in evil and its results. The question is thought-provoking, but not critical to your main point, so don't get lost in it!

Question 5. *Wow!*

Question 6. This "one flesh" union, where a man and woman leave their parents and "become one flesh" is a graphic picture of unity on every level, so that a new family is created. It involves union physically, emotionally and spiritually. There's also a quote about this whole-person union in the "User's Guide" section.

Question 9. See the "Challenge" section.

Final comment. This discussion is fairly long. So you may want to end with the questions under the "Challenge" section; encourage group members to look at part two of the story and the "Self-Reflection" question on their own. In general, it will help if every one of the group members has a guide to refer to outside of group time.

Session Two. Is There Help for Sexual Mistakes & Regrets?
Luke 7:36-50.

Main point: Jesus wants to forgive our mistakes and heal the broken parts of our sexuality.

General note. The goal in this discussion is to help people see how loving and accepting Jesus is toward people who have made mistakes and failed. All he asks is that we admit we have struggles and commit to seeking God. As a matter of fact, God is much more welcoming to struggling people who ask for help and forgiveness than to self-righteous people who feel like they don't need help.

Video clip cue. The movie quote is 1 hour, 15 minutes, 30 seconds into the movie.

Questions 1-2. This woman loves Jesus a lot. Jesus had this kind of amazing influence on people who felt condemned or excluded by others.

Question 3. This is not a time to name names. Help people to personalize the interaction with the Pharisee. Sometimes people think God is like the self-righteous judgmental people they know. Nothing could be further from the truth.

Questions 4-5. These questions apply the passage to how we view God. It should be encouraging for people to see what God is like in light of how Jesus loves and forgives.

Question 6. *Faith* is another word for *trust.* It means putting our full weight on someone, and placing our full trust in another, in this case God. God isn't looking for us to work our way into God's good graces, but to trust God for the gift of forgiveness and love and relationship.

Final comment. The "Self-Reflection" questions in this discussion are very good questions to ask aloud.

Session Three. Is There Healing for Sexual Hurts?

Mark 5:24-34.

Main point. Since we have all been hurt at some point sexually, and we all struggle with our sense of worth at some point, we all need the kind of powerful love, forgiveness and public affirmation that Christ gives.

General note. The goal in this discussion is to have people see, with their minds and hearts, how deeply Jesus wants to address our struggles with self-worth and shame. Jesus wants to do that not just privately, but even publicly. This woman would not have been accepted back into society unless Jesus had stopped her and assured her publicly that she was healed. He wanted to heal her physically, but he also wanted to heal her emotionally, spiritually and socially. Jesus wants the same for our lives.

Video clip cue. The quote is 1 hour, 22 minutes and 30 seconds into the movie.

Question 1. Scandal, old age, obesity, disability, racial background, sexual orientation and social awkwardness are a few things that could be mentioned.

Question 2. Addictions to relationships, experiences or substances are all ways people try that end up increasing the sense of shame over the long haul. If you suggest this answer, it would be important to share vulnerably about how addiction has affected your life.

Question 4. See the comment in the general note.

Question 7. Here you could share personally about how Jesus has helped you in your own sense of shame or self-worth.

Self-Reflection. The self-reflection questions are good to discuss at the end, but it is important to give people freedom to share or not share the area they struggle with specifically. You can give them freedom to share or not share their struggle, but still ask the question about what Jesus might be saying to them.

Session Four. Is There Hope for Sexual Struggles?

Matthew 5:27-32; 7:1-11.

Main point. Since we all struggle with sexual urges and needs, and some of us struggle with powerful addictive tendencies, we would all be helped by the kind of strength and perspective that Christ gives.

General note. In this discussion, you are not telling people what is right and wrong, and you are not defining what temptation is for them. But you are working with their own sense of right and wrong in order to help them turn toward God in their struggle.

Video clip cue. The quote is 12 minutes and 30 seconds into the movie.

Going Deeper. This segment is especially important in helping people think about their own struggles. So unlike most sessions, the "Going Deeper" segment is very important for you to read and then to discuss, using the question at the end of that segment.

Question 1. Lust is self-centered desire. Sexual lust is the search for our own gratification without the love for the other person that motivates us to seek that person's best. Too often, sex today can be merely an exercise in self-gratification.

Question 3. Jesus may be using hyperbole or exaggeration in order to get through to his listeners. They thought adultery was one of the worst sins, but they winked at anything short of adultery. In that culture, men were free to divorce for any reason (even for burning the toast!). Then they took some other wife. And women were trapped, unable to do the same. Jesus was trying to expose the hypocrisy of these men through his use of exaggeration.

Question 4. Jesus is challenging judgmental, hypocritical people in both passages. In the adultery passage, he challenges people who condemn adulterers and yet are filled with lust (that is, self-centered sexual desire) themselves. In the passage on judging others, Jesus confronts people who judge others harshly but judge themselves kindly.

Question 7. This is an ideal time to share a personal struggle and way that you pray to God.

Self-Reflection. The question about how people may need to begin to go God's way in their sexual choices is a good question to end with.

Session Five. Is Premarital Sex Right If You Care for the Person?
1 Corinthians 6:12-20.

Main point. Sex has been given so that it works right when there is also intimacy and commitment. Being sex mates and being soul mates was intended to go together. This kind of soul connection and sexual union happens best in lifelong, committed, monogamous marriage.

General note. This discussion is the most direct and challenging one in the guide. You want people to be challenged and reflect on whether or not they are willing to go God's way in their sexual choices.

Video clip cue. The quote is 1 hour, 20 minutes and 30 seconds into the movie.

Question 1. Paul's motive for having good boundaries and limits in his life is that he wants to be truly free and not controlled by his needs and desires and addictions. If you can, share an experience of coming to understand the attractiveness of this kind of freedom. People today think freedom means not having any boundaries.

Question 5. Sex affects our bodies and even the core of who we are in an especially intimate and profound way. The impact of sex on our soul and psyche, for good or bad, is immense.

Question 6. Some of the consequences include increasing the pain and damage of breakups, becoming addicted to sexual experiences, betraying and hurting people we love and are committed to in the case of adultery, and adding issues of comparison and memories of intense prior sexual experiences to present relationships. We can also become much more attached to people than they are to us, and sex can intensify that attachment. Sex can also replace conversation and friendship in ways that confuse us about how deep a relationship is and how compatible we are with another person. Obviously you want others to think about these consequences. But you may also want to share a personal story or refer to some of the stories in the guide to raise the consequences people don't mention.

Self-Reflection. Spend some time sharing the costs and benefits of going God's way in our sexual choices from the "Self-Reflection" section. Since this is session five, and you have met as a group for a number of weeks, you should have enough trust to be able to encourage people to be fairly honest.

Session Six. How Do I Find Sexual Integrity & Fulfillment?

John 4:1-26, 39.

Main point. Hope for sexual sanity, integrity and fulfillment starts with a commitment to Christ and to God.

General note. Your main goal in this study is to give people an opportunity to ask God to come into the center of their lives and be their forgiver, healer and leader. Even if that's not where they are at, the discussion will give them a very good idea of how to respond to God if they want to later.

Video clip cue. The quote is 1 hour, 29 minutes and 25 seconds into the movie.

Question 1. In Middle Eastern culture, eating and drinking together is a sign of hospitality and equality. In addition, Jesus asks the woman for her help, which a Jewish man is not ever supposed to do. It violates the cultural and sexual boundaries of the day. That's why the woman is so surprised and so intrigued.

Question 3. Water, especially in the Middle Eastern desert areas, is a symbol for life. Jesus is offering eternal life, starting now. John 17:3, where Jesus defines eternal life as knowing God, and John 10:10, where Jesus says that he came that we might have life to the full are related ideas.

Question 4. Jesus knows all about the woman's mixed past, but also treats her with great respect by addressing her and asking for her help. This combination of knowing her worst secrets and yet treating her with deep care was irresistible for the woman.

Question 5. It would be good to share about a person who knows you, accepts you and calls out your best.

Question 6. It's not where you worship or what rituals you use, but it's your heart that God cares about.

Question 7. Share about a time God spoke to you or led you or encouraged you when you were down or in crisis.

Final comments. Give people an opportunity to respond aloud to the questions in the self-reflection section. If any group members want to respond and ask God into the center of their lives, and there is a lot of trust, you can even have them respond in the group. Or you may want to offer to meet with them one on one later. You can ask them if they want your help in responding to God. If they want your help, you can lead them in responding to God, using the prayer at the end of the study to prompt them. Let them know that you will prompt them, and give them opportunity to use their own words to respond to God. Start by praying a simple prayer of thanks that the person wants to respond to God. You can then encourage them to pray through the outline that follows session six.

"Admit in your own words that you have replaced God at the center with other things and people." Then give them time to do that silently or aloud.

"Accept Jesus' death on the cross for your sins." And then give them time to do that silently or aloud.

"Ask Jesus into the center of your life, and commit yourself to him as your forgiver, healer and leader." Then give them time to do that silently or aloud.

Finally, give thanks to God for their response, and pray for their relationship with God.

Then celebrate. Make sure to let them know that they may not feel different. But show them from Scripture (for example, Revelation 3:20) that Jesus promises to come in when we ask. Then give them the booklet *My Heart—Christ's Home*, and offer to meet with them later to talk about it.

You can also give them the option of responding to God on their own. It will help them if you can give them an explanatory booklet like *Circles of Belonging* if they want to respond on their own.

Finally, you will want to discuss with the group if they want to keep on meeting, and if so, what they want to discuss. You may find the other guides in this series helpful as a next step.

ACKNOWLEDGMENTS

I am grateful to the many partners, friends and coworkers who gave invaluable feedback in the preparation of this series. I am especially thankful to my seeking friends who always keep me honest.

I am also grateful to my editor, Cindy Bunch, who went above and beyond in the preparation of these guides. She not only edited them, but she fieldtested them, advocated for them and provided invaluable friendship and support along the way. Thanks also to Debbie Abbs, who provided research for many of the quotes I used.

I also want to thank Terry Erickson and Alec Hill in InterVarsity Christian Fellowship, Nancy Ortberg at Willow Creek Community Church and Doug Yonamine at the Willow Creek Association for their support of this project.

Rick Richardson

RESOURCES

Groups Investigating God® from InterVarsity Press

These guides are designed to provide a safe place to explore your ideas about God—whatever you believe. They are great for discussions with two or more people.

Finding God: How Can We Experience God? by Rick Richardson

There are lots of places to look for God—like relationships, nature, goodness and even our own pain. Sometimes we have the sense that God is real. But we can't quite get hold of it. And then we may wonder if God even wants to be found. This discussion guide explores various paths people have used to find God.

Following God: What Difference Does God Make? by Daniel Hill

Sometimes we try to separate our personal beliefs from our actions and choices. It's easier—and more fun. But eventually that way of life starts to feel hypocritical and dissatisfying. The sessions in this guide address real-life questions about what it means to follow God.

Sex: What's God Got to Do with It? by Rick Richardson

Perhaps you've thought or heard statements like these: "God doesn't like sex." "Christianity is sexually repressive and oppressive toward women and gays." Here's an opportunity to explore for yourself what the Bible actually says about sexuality.

Spirituality: What Does It Mean to Be Spiritual? by Rick Richardson

Many of us have tried various spiritual activities—meditation, nurturing our souls through listening to spiritual teachers, by reading books by those who seem to be ahead of us or by visiting church services or religious groups. Yet the search continues. And we feel empty. These sessions explore questions about finding spiritual satisfaction.

Other InterVarsity Press Resources

Circles of Belonging by Rick Richardson
A brief booklet offering a straightforward presentation of the message of Jesus that speaks deeply to the minds and hearts of people today.

Evangelism Outside the Box by Rick Richardson
If you are looking for ways to reach out to people and for help in responding to the new questions people are asking, this book will give you many helpful and practical ideas.

Jesus with Dirty Feet by Don Everts
An intriguing and compelling new look at Jesus that breaks through a lot of our stereotypes and misconceptions about who this man was and what he wanted.

My Heart—Christ's Home by Robert Boyd Munger
A booklet offering a simple, moving description of how we can make room in our hearts for God to become the center of our lives.

Other Resources

The Case for Christ and *The Case for Faith* by Lee Strobel
If you have tough questions about the rationality and credibility of Christian faith, these books are for you. Lee Strobel is a former atheist who looks at the questions that kept him from believing in God. Available from Zondervan Publishing.

GIG Training Guide
This guide to GIGs (Groups Investigating God) will give you immense help in starting and leading spiritual discussion groups for seekers. Available from InterVarsity Christian Fellowship at 1-866-265-4823 or <www.ivcf.org/store>.

Visit the InterVarsity Press website at <www.ivpress.com>.